THE PATH TO VICTORY

Delia Steinberg Guzmán

Contents

In spite of his FEARS,

the HERO

fights with COURAGE

for VICTORY.

Foreword

It is difficult to express the significance of a book like this, in which the author writes as she speaks and, for those of us who know her, speaks as she writes. But there is something even better: she thinks and feels as she speaks and writes.

Even if the chapters of this work were not conceived as a unitary text, but as a collection of articles published at different times, they have the quality of reflecting the unified vision of the writer. Whether using similar or different words, there is always a central axis around which her essential thought revolves. This is reassuring for her readers. It is not easy to find people who maintain their opinions in spite of circumstances, in spite of praise or criticism. It is not easy to find someone who remains rooted in their experiences while at the same time being flexible and open towards new and enriching ways of seeing the world.

As the author rightly explains, a life well lived is always heroic, because it contains an infinite number of difficulties that have to be constantly resolved. It is a simple, everyday heroism, which nevertheless requires an inner strength that never gives up.

In this work, heroism is presented as a wonderful art of overcoming oneself, which includes the possibility of falls and redemption, disappointments and learning. It is a heroism that is human and sensitive, rational and intuitive. The hero faces trials in a sensible way, without allowing himself to be deceived by false illusions or absurd fantasies. The book presents us with a hero who is great because he does not feel he is great, and is great because he does not feel he is small either. He simply is.

We are living in difficult times because of a lack of moral values and because we have to deal with a world in which all kinds of catastrophes often challenge our capacity to adapt, understand and stay strong within ourselves. However, the guidance provided by the thoughts presented here lead not to discouragement but to victory. Victory is to conquer and, especially, to conquer oneself.

I leave it to readers to discover the value of sincerity and simplicity. There is nothing that I can add.

Dr. Antonio Alzina

Introduction

History is an extraordinary showcase where different ideas have appeared and given rise to many different ways of life, like coloured crystals whose hues vary according to the light. Each age has its parameters, and human beings, on their endless path of searching, have been ruled by those models, which they have tried to follow and obey more than they would follow an idea from any other source. What is commonly accepted becomes like a law and, as time passes, some of the ideas that have been accepted become even more powerful than laws themselves.

In this way, success has always been a goal, even if it has not always been seen in the same light. What was considered success in one century, or just a few decades ago, may be seen today as a misplaced or outmoded longing, while other ambitions have taken the place of the previous ones. Only one thing remains constant: the desire for success, the need to succeed, the desire to be accepted and taken seriously by others, conforming to the law that makes the whole – us and the rest – a consistent mass from which standing out is not encouraged, even if it involves finding success by other routes.

The statistics fill pages upon pages in dozens of publications. It is very clear that in these times, success is defined by social prestige and financial power, which then give rise to other forms of power, and these in turn further increase prestige. It is true that academic research, science, the arts and knowledge in general have a place, but this is becoming smaller with time. Learning is a beautiful adornment which, with a few exceptions, goes together with the above-mentioned prestige of a solid social position backed by a respectable fortune.

It is not surprising, then, that young people in particular direct their aspirations towards those formulas for success if they want to be acknowledged in the societies they are living in and not join the long list of "marginalized" people. Today, the future is approached from that perspective: a vocation must be subject to a checklist of questions about its practicality in terms of power and wealth. Today there is a growing list of courses that can be studied with the intention of achieving a quick and profitable success and a social position that will be perceived as solid and lasting.

But not all that glitters is gold.

If these were truly formulas for succeeding in life, there ought to be many more happy people than we see. Unless we accept that success is one thing and happiness is another.

The same statistics that list all the successful people also reveal a progressive increase in the conditions of psychosis, depression, anguish, dissatisfaction, loneliness, aggression, boredom, corruption and many other psychological situations that make up the general pattern of "stress".

So, perhaps we should think of other types of success which, even if they don't conform to the commonly accepted types, may prove to be more effective.

We propose a few simple keys for achieving a more human success, in many different areas of life; a more stable victory, more in accordance with our dreams and aspirations.

It is clearly not enough to dream of victory. We need to act and we need to know how to develop a healthy activity based on will. We should not act just for the sake of it, but choose the best and most appropriate actions.

The old advice about knowing oneself is still applicable today; we will find it difficult to find a rewarding job if we don't know who we are or what our skills and abilities are. And once we know what they are, we need to train ourselves to develop them so that our activity will be useful to ourselves and others.

Whenever you undertake a task, do it well, not only for the reward you may receive, but also for the satisfaction of experiencing your own efficiency. Know how to be satisfied with what you obtain, and, at the same time, never rest on your laurels, always looking for a higher level of achievement.

Never allow yourself to feel crushed by problems, however difficult they may seem. On the contrary, exert your imagination in order to look for new avenues and solutions. Think of difficulties as challenges for your intelligence and your will. And in the worst case, turn failures into opportunities to make a new beginning.

Learn to take advantage of opportunities. Life is full of opportunities, but if we walk around with our eyes closed, we will never discover them. If we become imprisoned in our conflicts and constantly dwell on them, we will waste energy and never get out of that vicious cycle, ignoring the thousand doors which the supposed labyrinth was offering us.

Practise loving continuously, because this is the best way to understand others. Help others cheerfully and generously, which is the best way to feel at ease with yourself.

Search for the meaning of life and try to find the meaning of your own life. Nothing happens without a reason, and answers only come to those who look for them in the spirit of wisdom and with the courage of someone who is sure of victory.

Improve everything you do every day; improve everything around you without ever giving up. Put beauty into every corner; put light into every place - inner and outer - wherever you are.

Someone who succeeds in applying these few keys will be someone who is sure of themselves; a contented person insofar as contentment is possible for human beings. Someone who can achieve these things is truly successful. And even if no one admits it because it is not fashionable to do so everyone would like to attain this kind of success.

This short book is a homage to the brave, to all those who have the strength to keep going. Above all, to the brave who have no name, whether they be great or small, because no one knows them, and yet they are with us, they are all around us, they are everywhere in the world. They are the spirit of all progressive movement.

It is a homage to those who are in the world, to those who have made the world their home, regardless of difficulties. It is a homage to those who have learned to give things their proper value; the brightness of a stone, the leaf sprouting from a branch, the sounds of animals, the words of humans, the language of the gods.

It is a homage to the brave who always find a way out of the labyrinth: they keep walking, constantly looking for the door which will give them freedom. And they fall, they fall a thousand times and a thousand times they pick themselves up again, and every time they get up they are a little stronger.

It is a homage to those who have developed continuity, to those who have never lost their way, because their heart is a compass which always points north; to those who never lose their rhythm, because their heart is a drum beating time for them.

This is a homage to the brave who seek fraternity and harmony among human beings, even though all around them there is pain, terror and death.

It is a homage to those who stretch out their arms like a bridge, to those who do not experience it as a sacrifice and do not mind becoming a passage between the human and the divine.

This is a homage to those who always have the ability to bring us regeneration, to heal our wounds, to alleviate our sorrows, to give us a solution for everything. It is a homage to the Lords of Rebirth, who choose the hard and sharp weapon of wisdom to fight with, like a double-edged axe that can open up the minds of others, but above all opens up the mind of the one who wields it. It is a homage to the Lords of Wisdom.

It is a homage to the heroes of life, because it is very difficult to live. It is a homage to those who are interested in life above all else, and understand the need to fight as a way of protecting life. For in the heart of all human beings there is no war: there is life. In the heart of all human beings there is no war: there is eternity.

It is a homage, in short, to all the brave, to all the heroes, great and small, who do not know one another, either because they are very great or because they are very small, but who nevertheless are always going forward, above all when times are hard and difficult.

The Hero

What is a hero?

This term can be explained in several different ways.

- The hero is a demi-god, a being with a twofold nature, that is to say, he has a human part and a divine part both clearly manifested. The first brings him closer to all human beings, enabling him to understand them easily; it also leads him to commit human errors from time to time and to suffer as people in general suffer. The divine part urges him to use his strength to help everyone as much as he can, and even more.

Of course, there will always be a struggle in the human being between the two parts of his dual nature. The strictly human part will pull him down towards inertia and comfort, and will ask him to allow himself to be carried along by the current of existence, whether placid or turbulent. The divine part will urge him to scale the rungs of effort and sometimes pain, but this is glorious and clarifying for his soul.

But it is impossible to remain in such an intermediate state forever.

- The hero is the child of love.

We find the following in one of Plato's dialogues (*Cratylus,* or *On the Accuracy of Words,* translated by Benjamin Jowett):

> HERMOGENES: ... but what is the meaning of the word "hero"?
> SOCRATES: I think that there is no difficulty in explaining, for the name is not much altered, and signifies that they were born of love (...).
> Do you not know that the heroes are demigods? (...).
> All of them sprang either from the love of a God for a mortal woman, or of a mortal man for a Goddess.
> Think of the word in the old Attic, and you will see better that the name 'heros' is only a slight alteration of Eros, from whom the heroes sprang...

The love of the gods is not expressed only in the generation of physical life, in a child of flesh and blood. On the contrary, their offspring are psychological, mental and spiritual, and therefore more powerful and lasting. They can appear in the form of intuition, inspiration, a store of unsuspected strengths and energies.

The love of humans for their superior models is what leads them to become similar to them; it is the only force that will transform them into demigods, into heroes. And it is love that helps us to live in accordance with a new condition of the soul.

- A hero is someone who has gained due recognition for his feats, for his exceptional deeds, for his courage in difficult situations, for his ability to forge ahead at crucial moments, for not giving up where anyone else would have done so out of fear or desperation.

- A hero is a person who is recognized for his many qualities in the daily struggle for life, for which some very special weapons are necessary: the virtues, the human powers which normally lie beneath the surface, buried in the depths of the unconscious, or have not even been born yet.

- The hero recognizes himself when he recognizes the trials that Destiny offers him. When, instead of rejecting them and fearing them, he takes them on and prepares to live them, the hero has discovered the most important thing about himself. He knows what his human strengths are. And an ancestral shout from afar reminds him of his inner potentials, the latent forces that are waiting for a more or less immediate awakening. As J.A. Livraga wrote: "In spite of the many attempts to convince human beings that they can rise no higher than the human state, the hero is the expression of the individual who strives to rise above his limitations, who stretches his arms and his consciousness to reach the height of the divine. He is not a god, but he is something more than a man. He is not perfect, but he has learned to seek perfection. He is a hero in action, a wonderful intermediary between earth and heaven."

What is heroism?

It is to embark on a long journey to try to discover who we are.

Those of us who aspire to be heroes, even if we are still all too mortal, want to know the truth about ourselves.

Who am I? is the question which impels us to walk along the human path and, even more, on the heroic path. This question also contains within it the need to know, *Where do I come from?* and *Where I am going?*. They are the three moments of all identity.

Identity is not to find something which is the same as or identical to ourselves in our present state. It is both simpler and more difficult: it is to find ourselves. We are not looking for the shadow we cast in the world, but for the reality which was able to cast that shadow. Today, yesterday and tomorrow.

To recognize ourselves is to know who we are now, without any false masks. This is something that carries with it a lot of the past - where we come from - and of the future - where we are going. To know who we are is to own a piece of time.

Heroism is to know what is expected of us.

However hard it may be - and this is the basis of the heroic being - we are expected to emerge victorious from the trials we have to face. What is expected is our heroic deed.

Who is expecting it? Oneself, destiny, life which is guiding us - the "infinite orphans", that part of humanity that remains helpless and defenceless in the face of the vicissitudes of existence - with immense patience and kindness.

Heroism is precisely that effort which brings our will, love and intelligence into play, so that we can put ourselves at the service of humanity, in the name of all that is sacred and for the benefit of all those who need us, from the simplest beings to our planet Earth. It is the generosity that expresses itself in extraordinary actions.

No one will demand of us an absolute victory, only that we should continue with what our ancestors began and leave some very clear footprints behind us, so that those who come after us can find them and follow them, in the sure knowledge that they have found the path of success.

We can all be heroic. We only need our piece of time and our piece of success.

Can we all be heroes?

To some extent, we can all achieve it.

- We all share a dual nature. And although it may not be as clear-cut as it is with the real heroes, we are often aware when there is an urge at work in us which can be called "animalistic"; and when, on the other hand, the soul rises up to come into contact with the sacred. It is up to us, then, to make the effort to keep our divine nature more active and to make our victory over our animal reactions more apparent.

- We have all achieved some small feat which makes our lives more elevated. In the worst of cases, we imagine it, which is the expression of an unfulfilled desire. We have all overcome - or wanted to overcome - one or several exceptional situations. It is up to us to make the effort to achieve real feats, and more of them. Obviously, our feats will be at our own level, but it is also true that there is nothing to stop us from growing in stature. Can we put a limit to human evolution? Only the vain believe that a higher evolutionary state can never be attained.

- We all have some virtue, whether latent or expressed. There is no one who has no positive aspects in their personality. It is up to us to make the effort to develop our latent powers, to make space for them in our life and to polish the virtues we already possess.

- We can all overcome death. Partly, because we can all write a few lines in the great book of history and so earn a piece of memory in time. Partly because, alive or dead, we can continue to accompany the people we love. And partly, finally, because the development of consciousness allows us to perceive our own immortality naturally, which is the most important thing, whether others recognize it or not.

One of the most outstanding characteristics of the hero is that he can work in the short, medium and long term, but without ever stopping. His vision is not limited to the present and his action is not the result of a momentary impulse. He can progress day by day, year by year, decade by decade, without losing his patience or enthusiasm.

He knows that any work that is aimed at the future has to begin with himself, since he cannot demand anything from others unless he has first demonstrated his own measure of effort and success.

The true hero recognizes the true meaning of power. Power is not a kind of immunity that allows us to exercise control over others, but the strength that is required to become better every day. All power comes from within, although it is not enough just to have ideas about what power may be considered to be; true power arises from the inner being, which becomes powerful as it perfects itself.

And so begins the hero's great journey. To go on a journey is to travel along a path.

The hero's journey

All heroes are great travellers. Some make great inner journeys without moving from where they are. Others travel immense distances to reach their goal.

The hero does not necessarily go out in search of new lands, or new worlds, eager to explore and possess what is closer or further away from him; he knows that first he must emerge victorious from the search for and conquest of himself.

In this way, heroes have to travel in order to achieve their heroic status. Their paths may appear to be many and varied, but the goal is always the same: self-conquest through the passing of trials; self-mastery in order to serve others.

The path is neither long nor short. It is simply the right way for the hero to conquer his higher condition, so that no chain can drag him back to forgetfulness, to the lack of memory which results in error. The path has no end in sight, as time has no end.

What the hero does is to walk through time with a constantly renewed consciousness, because he is a favourite child of time. He advances along its eternal paths, tracing upward-moving spirals. His principal victory is to never stop. He does not think about resting or about the end of the journey, but plunges into the stream of time and lives in harmony with the rhythm of that hidden heart of history.

The hero does not fight against time. That is why he does not grow old. He is always young. That is why he does not die, even if he is destroyed by the most terrible weapons, because his memory continues to beat in unison with life. He is always alive.

The hero does not fight against time. He does not look back, nor does he try anxiously to glimpse what lies far beyond the steps he is taking. He generates the future minute by minute, as he advances.

The hero does not fight against time. That is why he transcends time and his example endures down through the ages, becoming a model to follow, an incentive and a hope for those who come after him.

Today is yesterday and it is also tomorrow. Today is about walking.

When the future hero sets out on his first journey, the whole path lies in front of him and all the trials are yet to come. He has the intuition that the path will be complex, but he will not know for certain until he has undergone his first experiences.

The most important thing is the traveller.

The traveller has to be engaged in every step he takes with his whole being. He cannot have his memory or his feelings stuck in the past, because then his feet will become immobilized. He is both the vehicle and the one who is carried in the vehicle.

He must recognize each stretch of the road and calculate the similarities and differences between the place he is at and the place he has left. In this way, he will become increasingly able to calculate the possibilities he will find at the next stop.

His journey has resting places, but it never ends. Wherever he stops, he evaluates his experiences. He examines the trials he has overcome and also those he will have to reattempt. He repacks his belongings, restores his energy, recovers his cheerfulness and, at the same time, reduces his sorrows and sets out again towards the conquest.

As time passes, the aspirant grows more and more into a hero. His knowledge has increased. He can see how far he has travelled, although he does not worry about how far he still has to go. What matters is what has been done, because that is where his merits lie. The distances are great, but not infinite; the horizon is wide, but not hazy. The trials are difficult, but he has already had successes that will help him to overcome new difficulties with greater skill.

Now he is a traveller and not only an adventurer.

Now he knows what it means to travel, although he has not completed the journey.

The hero walks on an ascending path, as if climbing a ladder. He can sense the top of the ladder; but what he is concentrating on at each moment is the next rung. His intuition tells him that the last rung leads to heaven – to the heaven of each one in their own degree – but it is not heaven that concerns him, only how he can reach it without losing the ground he has gained, without falling backwards.

On his journey he gets to know lands different from those that witnessed his birth, undreamed-of landscapes, but they all become part of his world. He is faced with vicissitudes and situations that are difficult to gauge, but all of them provide him with new weapons. He meets people whom he will come to love or hate, but all of them give him opportunities for learning. Sometimes he is welcomed and at other times he is rejected, but in either case he understands that the secret lies in continuing on his path.

If the voice of the hero echoes in some corner of your heart, you will know that this journey is unavoidable. That anyone who wishes to reach the goal must move towards it. That heaven is won by lifting one's feet off the ground. That the way may appear to be difficult and exhausting, but the more you advance the more strength arises within you and the weaker the darkness that hinders your progress becomes, while tiredness is replaced by enthusiasm.

All of us carry within us a more or less awakened hero. All of us can hear his call. All of us who seek knowledge for the love of wisdom know that, almost without noticing it, we have started on a journey. On that journey we will encounter a series of trials.

The trials

All heroes face many trials throughout their existence, some more difficult than others.

Some of these trials attract our attention because they involve terrible monsters that have to be vanquished. Sometimes they announce their appearance, at other times they take us by surprise. Their mask is ugliness, violence, the threat to survival; in short, fear in all its forms.

But what do these monsters really represent?

Are we to think that, when the heroes pass by, they awaken ancient, evil beings that were supposed to have disappeared or had been forgotten forever?

This is not possible. Behind the symbols, we see two types of monsters to overcome.

THE MONSTERS OF EVIL

All human beings, whether they are heroes or not, carry with them a considerable number of sorrows, fears, unresolved conflicts, anxieties, doubts…

When they set out on their valiant journey, old psychological elements that were previously hidden, take shape. What shape? The shape of monsters.

They are as ugly as the space they occupy in the soul, as ugly as the fear and paralysis they cause, as ugly as the time they steal from other possibilities of being more active in a better way.

At other times, the monsters are new. Every hero has to fight against his old shadows, but he also has to overcome new difficulties that will enable him to grow.

But old or new, they all have a terrifying and beastly appearance.

Those who have not yet had the courage to achieve the condition of heroes drag these monsters around with them, trying to hide them, pretending to be indifferent to them, postponing having to confront them, or simply putting up with their existence without looking for solutions. The easiest and most usual way out is to blame the existence of these beasts on others, or on the cruelty of life.

Heroes, on the other hand, face up to them. At least, they take the decision to confront them.

The hero's battle against monsters is the hero's battle against his own imperfections, against his weaknesses, against his more mundane aspects that prevent him from earning his share of divinity.

In the symbolic tales the hero emerges battered and bruised, but always victorious. This is the natural way of things. It is the only way to earn the status of a human being who is advancing towards the future.

THE MONSTERS OF GOOD

There is another type of monster which, while appearing to be terrifying, is not bad. Behind its horrific mask, precious treasures of knowledge lie hidden, which have to be won through effort and by mastering our fears.

Every time the hero goes into a labyrinth, into a cave, into a dark and lonely lair, in order to kill some horrifying being of which he knows nothing, in reality he is facing his own fear. When in the end he finds himself in the presence of the feared monster, when finally he has removed the blindfold from his eyes, he discovers that, behind the vision of ugliness and cruelty, there was what he had always longed for: wisdom and power over himself.

The seeker of wisdom knows deep down that he must leave behind the life he has been leading until now. Ignorance and wisdom do not see existence in the same way, and this leads to substantial changes which are equivalent to the death of old and bad habits, harmful ways of living, unjustified fears. Something dies, yes, but what is born is much better.

Companions and solitude

To have companions is one of the distinctive characteristics of the hero. It is not easy to explain, but everyone who has faced and overcome difficult situations is somehow aware of this reality: that we are not alone.

The companions of the hero play a fundamental role, because the hero rarely embarks on his adventures alone. He travels along the paths of life in the company of those who have to go through similar, though not always identical, situations.

Sometimes there are many companions, because the hero's story - an expansion of the symbol - takes place in the context of a great war in which everyone fights shoulder to shoulder. At other times there is only one companion: the great friend, the only one, the special and long-awaited friend with whom the hero shares his decisive trials. And even though there may be separation, those earthly separations can never break a bond that goes beyond life and crosses the barriers of death.

The hero's companions are the proof that the hero is not alone, even though he goes through the experience of his trials in solitude. The companions are the living symbol of humanity, which is much more than the sum of different human beings. They are the symbol of heroism, which is much more than a single hero.

Yes, he has companions, but the hero is destined to go through his great trials alone; and yet, at the same time, he has to share them with his companions. Solitude and companionship are not mutually exclusive, but each has its proper time and value.

Solitude is the fertile ground in which the individuality of the immortal soul develops. Each soul has its particular qualities, its special karmic seeds[1], its open doors or opportunities. In this case, the individual aspect is untransferable. Although human beings are like drops in the ocean, each drop retains its distinctive quality.

It is impossible to arrive at the "I am", without going through the necessary trials to distinguish that individuality which has travelled through aeons in time and space before taking up its present position in the scheme of evolution.

It is not, therefore, a physical solitude or an aloofness from other beings. It is not about separating oneself from life or its conditions. It is an inner solitude, in which it is up to each individual to deal with their own questions and answers, just as the actions we take and their consequences are our own responsibility. It is the solitude of hell or that of the inner temple, the solitude of the storm or of peace, in which external circumstances have little or no influence.

It is the solitude of the consciousness which takes responsibility for itself, without justifications or excuses. Either one is, or one is not. And that can only be experienced in solitude. In the heroic solitude of one who can be happy in these conditions, which he recognizes as the best means of earning his place among the victors.

1 Karma is the law of retribution or cause and effect. Generally speaking, it refers to the fact that every action, feeling or thought has consequences that determine our present and future lives.

When the hero falls

As heroes are the children of both gods and men, that twofold nature means that throughout their lives there are moments of divine greatness and others of human weakness. When the latter prevail, the heroes suffer momentary falls. They are not definitive falls; nor do they last for too long, but they are falls all the same and bring with them their inevitable burden of pain.

Why do heroes fall?

We are not going to discuss the exceptional cases where some of them pretend to be in a moment of crisis as a strategy for defeating their enemy. There are very few Achilleses[2] in history...

We are interested in the other cases, those of genuine crisis, as reflected in the Bhagavad Gita[3] when Arjuna[4] throws down his bow, falls to the floor of his chariot and decides not to fight. That moment of weakness is one of the fundamental experiences which has to be overcome by every hero and by every human being who wants to make their life a ladder of ascension, rather than a featureless plain.

Heroes fall because they are partly human.

Because their human part keeps them in a state of constant struggle between their earthly condition and the other, higher condition, which makes greater demands on them and creates difficulties in every part of the personality.

---

2 Achilles was one of the heroes of the Trojan War. The story goes that an oracle offered him the choice between a long and uneventful life and a short but glorious one. He chose the latter.

3 The Bhagavad Gita, or *Song of the Master*, is one of the most important texts of ancient India. It forms part of the great epic, the Mahabharata.

4 Together with the god Krishna, Arjuna is the hero and protagonist of the Mahabharata.

Because sometimes the fight is very hard and our endurance is not so strong.

Because sometimes a drop appears which makes the cup overflow…

Because it is necessary to know the depths of hell in order to value the heights of heaven.

Because it is necessary to know oneself, one's own weak points, rather than trusting blindly in success without obstacles.

How are these falls expressed?

In many ways, but with a common background. The complaints become more intense, it seems that the whole building is collapsing and yet, behind the creaking timbers and the complaints, the soul is intact. It is simply crying.

Once again, the example of Arjuna is the most useful one for understanding the situation of the hero when he falls. The enemy appears to be larger than he is. The hero thinks his strengths are less than they are. He appears to be convinced that the battle is already lost even before it has started. He undervalues his own worth and at the same time justifies his weakness. He thinks that if he abandons the battle he will find peace, in exchange for the terrible anguish he is suffering at that moment.

Arjuna, however, is willing to listen to his teacher Krishna. Even more: he needs to listen to him, he needs his advice, he needs someone to restore his confidence in himself and provide him with new weapons so that he can carry on without losing heart. His complaints are more against himself than against the difficulty of the trials he has to bear and overcome.

In other cases, there are heroes whose personalities are almost destroyed, who fall into vegetative states from which it seems that they will never be able to recover, who fall into depravity in an attempt to destroy themselves and laugh at their own weakness. But this is all a superficial veneer and the smallest spark of real fire is enough to make them wake up from their nightmare and get back on their feet again.

How does the hero get up again?

A fallen hero is a man who is asleep; he is lying in a terrible half-sleep from which he does not want to awake; or rather, he wants to come out of it with the help of someone who has the strength that he lacks at that moment.

The hero does not need someone to lift him up completely. That would humiliate him and would make him fall again, because he would discover that he has not moved by his own willpower. The hero just needs an initial push, a ray of light to show him his state of darkness, the right teaching to dissolve his momentary weakness, an achievable hope to restore his energy, a powerful memory to enable him to recognize himself, to recover and take up the path again where he had left off.

It may seem that the hero, when he falls, goes backwards. It is an illusion of the senses, above all of the mind. The backward movement - if there is one - is a review of the path that was badly mapped out, and the setting of a new speed in order to make up for the lost time. The backward movement is a taking stock, it is to see what was not seen before, to have a better knowledge of one's own values and the dangerous curves of one's destiny.

A hero gets up with courage.

A hero gets up without false shame, because no one is free from falling.

A hero gets up quickly, with the flexibility of the inner youth who never died, because he has left behind him the state into which he had fallen.

A hero gets up with more strength, with more enthusiasm, with more serenity, with a greater sense of reality.

To put it simply: when a hero gets up, he is even more of a hero.

Conquests

A hero knows that he has to earn his possessions, that it is his merits that bring him victory, and he fights for everything he wants to obtain.

Although many of our human characteristics might seem to be gifts from destiny or from nature, they have cost us many efforts which we have now forgotten.

Our Self is the child of struggle. To live is a struggle. To die is also a struggle.

Life is not a gift. It is a permanent battle and each thing that is obtained is a conquest. Someone who knows how to live is a hero, even if they do not use that word.

Conquest is what gives value to things. Persistent effort bestows a special price on each of our possessions, which for that very reason are always possessions, even if they have made us experience the taste of pain.

Struggle shows us who we truly are. We know what we are capable of, and what level we can reach, by going beyond our own limits.

Conquest makes us understand that there are things that can

be lost, but there are other things that will be ours for the rest of our lives. It makes us distinguish between what has a relative value and what has a permanent value.

The spirit of conquest overcomes the fear of life and its difficulties because it develops the capacity to choose solutions and to decide on our own choices.

Struggle overcomes the fear of death, because when someone has learned how to live and how to overcome the natural difficulties of life, they know that they will also be able to cross that new threshold naturally.

Struggle makes us strong, makes us victorious, enthusiastic. It gives us confidence in ourselves, the ability to trust others and relate to them, to recognize all the good that we find at every step we take.

Truly, someone who knows how to struggle knows how to value each detail of life and knows what it means to be brave. They know their own value and the value of things. They are worthy of their life and the conquests obtained throughout their life.

There is no greater merit than an awakened consciousness. And this awakening is the result of many blows, of many wounds, and of the effort to heal the wounds and to recover from the blows, while at the same time creating new weapons so as not to repeat the same mistakes again. The shadow of the conquered pain is what brings out the brightness of a lasting happiness.

PERENNIAL YOUTH

This is the great conquest of the hero.

Representations in paintings and sculptures, reliefs on ancient buildings and images created by different artists, all show heroes and heroines with an appearance of permanent youth.

Perhaps this is due to the timeless genius of those works of art, which do not admit the ageing of features. But the most likely explanation is that there has always been a desire to emphasize the special features of youth.

Heroes are capable of performing one feat after another, suffering numerous setbacks and even serious injuries which bring them close to death; but they never cease to be young. The years pass by, adventures come and go and the hero preserves the same power, as if time were no more than a gentle wind brushing over his skin.

One influencing factor may be that myths also never grow old. But it is very likely that there are other deeper symbols involved.

What is always evident is the eternal youth of the heroes, in whom the strongest feature is always the magnetic power of a physical and spiritual strength that nothing can destroy.

As long as the hero remembers his spiritual origins, as long as earthly life does not make him forget his immortal roots, he will remain young, strong and courageous for all the days of his life, however long that may be.

Someone who recognizes his dual nature - spiritual and material - and the primacy of the former over the latter, is a hero who distinguishes his divine part from his human part. If he remains faithful to his spiritual nature and does not allow himself to be trapped by strictly material needs, as if they were the only reason for existence, he has found a source of unchanging youth. The enduring nature of the spirit is transmitted to his attitudes on all the planes of life, and even to his actual physical presence.

This youthfulness - which distinguishes gods and heroes and is so sought after by humans - is an inner energy which is expressed in a constant vitality, an always dynamic sensibility and a mind alert to every detail. It is a youthfulness which is nourished by a healthy morality, an inexhaustible capacity for improving oneself, for perceiving the laws that govern nature and for entering into contact with all beings.

Our human heroism consists in discovering our own energy so that we can conquer time and live in continual action.

It is not so difficult to find it.

It is enough if we know how to feel, by choosing the elements that will help us to maintain a healthy sensitivity, that is, by refusing entry to all the dark and negative emotions.

It is enough if we know how to think, by keeping the consciousness active with elevated occupations and studies, avoiding the gaps through which confused and destructive ideas might surreptitiously gain entry.

It is enough if we know that we are part of nature, if we understand and respect its laws; by acting in this way, we will make room for a natural morality and a perception of the sacred that will enrich us minute by minute.

It is enough if we get up every day with renewed enthusiasm, facing whatever we have to do - however routine it may seem to us - as if it were the most attractive of adventures.

It is enough if we have high aspirations and devote ourselves to noble ideals; it is enough if we serve others more than our own selfish desires.

It is enough if we observe these simple rules of life, for then eternal youth will become our inseparable companion. The companion of the true hero. The great conquest of the hero.

JUSTICE

The hero loves Justice, he searches for it by every means and exercises his courage to make it reign in the world. Because he applies justice to himself, he dares to propose it to others.

Justice is the virtue that connects so many others: "Justice (...) is not limited to the external actions of the human being, but also applies to man's inner action upon himself and the principles within him (...) establishing a veritable order within himself, inducing him to rule himself, to discipline himself and to be his own friend." (Plato, *The Republic*).

If we accept that justice is to give to each person what is due to them according to their acts and nature, then the hero must know both the laws of nature and the different human natures, in order to distinguish what is appropriate for each individual, without upsetting the general equilibrium.

It is evident that anger is the mirror of the anti-hero. The hero does not get angry, he arms himself with bravery, with temperance and, thus protected, he preserves goodness and truth. The hero recognizes merits wherever he finds them and only despises injustice, falseness, ostentatious pride, and cruelty.

Justice is also a great conquest for the hero.

The end of the path

We would like to find a happy ending where the hero is victorious, the battles and sorrows are over and he can rest after achieving his goal. It would be comforting to think that, at some point, the path ends and the trials come to an end.

But if we gave in to such desires, we would lose touch with the true hero.

Although at times truth can be hard, it is preferable to face it. As real heroes do. And the truth is that the trials do not end, nor does the pain by which they force us to re-evaluate our lives. The truth is that a victory is very important, but it does not mark a final end, only the beginning of another battle. The only kind of rest is movement in search of harmony.

One rung leads to another, one trial leads to the next. There is no complete rest, or at least not for now. As long as the hero has a divine part and another human part, he will have to continue along his way. Life will present him with different cycles as opportunities for growth. The human part will be gradually polished, like a precious stone, and will begin to shine as it reflects its divine nature. But there will always be difficulties to overcome and deeds to perform. Rest will be little more than a sweet respite, a high point on the path when the soul must remain alert so that it does not lose the direction that leads to the next goal.

When the hero thinks he has reached his destination, he will discover that he has only reached the end of a stage. And new doors will open before him. He will no longer be attacked by ancient monsters, because they will have been defeated; all the evils arising from ignorance will have vanished like shadows. Now he will have to face the monsters of knowledge, to recognize the small truths little by little and to use them to construct a solid ladder that will lead him to wisdom.

Fears

One of the psychological factors that slow down or even stop the development of the human being, in all his aspects, is fear.

Although we recognize fear as a heavy emotion that arises from the psyche, it is evident that its field of action is not limited to that plane. When fear descends, it paralyzes the body; when it ascends, it paralyzes the mind; and, in its own house, it cools down the best sentiments, while at the same time giving monstrous proportions to other more negative emotions.

We all feel fear, or have felt it once, or are afraid of experiencing it again. Those who deny this are only revealing their fear, though under the disguise of vanity. The problem is not whether we feel or have felt fear, but what we can do to ensure that this emotion does not prevent us from walking along the path.

Even the greatest of heroes feel fear. Otherwise, they would have lost an intrinsic part of their human condition. All human beings experience fear on certain occasions and for different reasons.

What distinguishes the hero from someone who has not yet become one is that the hero rises above his fear. Without ceasing to feel it, he can rise to a higher level and from there can master his actions. Even master his fears.

There are many fears, as many as there are individuals, and each person's fears will reflect their own characteristics. Generally speaking, however, all these fears can be reduced to just a few categories: fear of failure in all senses, fear of one's own personality with its weaknesses and one's inability to master them, and fear of pain in all its aspects.

As we can see, fears originate in ourselves, in our emotions and in a certain destructive reasoning process that prevents us from acting in an appropriate way. It is precisely those inner, psychological fears that paralyze human beings and cause them to get stuck at a certain point on the path, making them afraid of walking and going forward. It is very rare to hear people admit that they are afraid of external factors or people, because they soon realize that the threat does not come so much from outside as from within. It is the inner fear that makes external factors frightening.

Fear of failure

Regardless of age, we never master to perfection everything we would like to know and understand; we don't even manage to master ourselves. And whenever we have achieved something, time has shown us that our conquest was not lasting and that a small obstacle was enough to make us lose what we thought we had gained. That sense of insecurity - which is a form of ignorance - gradually saps our strength, unless we remove the mask under which it is hiding and decide, with will and constancy, to fight it. We need to reflect more and assimilate the results of those reflections on a deep level, putting them into practice every day, making our philosophy a real way of life; because no one becomes an expert in a day or becomes an adult in just a few months. Philosophy needs to be applied patiently and attentively, and we need to place our feet firmly on each rung of the ladder before climbing up to the next. It is not simply about climbing up to the next rung, but making sure we are stable on the rung we are on.

The more we know - with the deep and inner knowing of philosophy - the less fear and insecurity we will experience.

Fear of failure is expressed in many ways: failing as an idealist, not measuring up, not being up to the demands or circumstances; not fulfilling one's dreams or just letting them die; losing one's hopes, one's enthusiasm, and so on.

Fear of failure is a failure to take the necessary action to achieve success. Before undertaking anything, the mind and the emotions present us with the terrible possibility of failure and, rather than assume that risk, we choose an even greater risk, which is that of failing anyway, because where nothing is ventured, nothing is gained.

What is failure? Little more than a mistake, because if we look at the inevitable evolution of life, there are no absolute failures. All mistakes can be corrected, especially if they are examined calmly and recognized sincerely and in time.

Of course, without a spirit of risk-taking, there will not be the necessary equanimity to accept and learn from our mistakes. To act is a risk: we may, or may not, obtain good results; and if we don't, we can try to find a new way of rectifying the mistakes. But if nothing is risked - even if the risk is no more than that noble human attitude of being prepared to make mistakes, to listen to good advice and to apply that advice - then no results, either good or bad, will be obtained.

All that will be left will be the bitter taste of the fear of failure, before we have even tried anything or after a first failed attempt. Action dispels failure.

However hard it may sound, you only fail if you want to fail. On the path of learning there is nothing to "measure up to" except one's own standards and we need only "be up to" the height we can reach. Instead of allowing fear as an emotion and failure as an idea to enter our being, we should propose the opposite: there is no such thing as failure, only mistakes, and every mistake can be corrected and redeemed. Someone who thinks like that is unlikely to give in to the fear of not achieving what they want, of losing ground in the battle to conquer oneself.

Fear of oneself

Fear of oneself is hidden in that "dark part" that lies in the deep and dimly lit part of the consciousness. It is not an evil darkness; it is ignorance. Consequently, passions have more power there than reason, weakness than courage, selfishness than generosity. The daily problems of survival, of personal and romantic relationships, become mountains that seem almost impossible to climb and, as if that were not enough, they also prevent us from seeing the spiritual realities; they become the only or the most important realities.

Let us begin by remembering that, for the traveller on the path of life, love of wisdom is fundamental; and not only love, but also the gradual conquest of wisdom. There is no point complaining about one's own weaknesses, about the fear of not being able to make it through difficult times; rather, we need to shine a light on those weaknesses so that we can get to know them well. At the same time, we need to develop our potentials, which we must also learn to find. No human being is devoid of positive qualities, however latent they may be.

Problems are not there to crush us, but to test our ability to go beyond our limits. And if we are not continually trying out ways of moving forward, even in the worst circumstances, fear will grow ever stronger, and our lack of confidence will increase in proportion.

Every problem has a solution, and we have to find it. What we cannot expect is a perfect or ultimate solution. The perfect and the ultimate are not plants of this world. There are more or less good solutions that can help us keep walking; later on, it may be possible to improve on them or adapt them if new problems appear, which is an inevitable feature of the school of life.

But we have to try things out, we have to use our own strengths, we have to dare to begin and not give way in the face of failures. Like everything that involves learning, it is necessary to try things out, to make mistakes and corrections.

Fear of oneself reflects a lack of will to work on oneself. It is to allow our involuntary impulses to win the battle rather than face them. By acting and facing difficult situations over and over again, one develops willpower, the discipline of action, inner security and self-confidence.

Fear of the unknown is another of the faces of fear. As the broad vista of philosophy gradually opens up before us, we begin to perceive the immensity of what is still to be known. But that is a natural attitude of the philosopher, and was precisely the attitude that led Socrates to say, "I only know that I know nothing". To know something is to become aware of what we still have to learn; but that is no justification for being afraid of what we don't yet know.

Our universe is a coherent and correlated unity. The unknown may be greater, broader, higher, more wonderful, more powerful or more luminous than what we know, but it will never be absolutely different. We should move towards the unknown, that is, towards what we still have to learn, not with fear, but with the spiritual joy of someone who is gradually discovering the unexplored laws of nature and the latent powers in the human being.

Fear of pain

Fear of pain, whether physical or psychological, is an acknowledgement of our weakness... and a sure way of increasing the pain, because the more afraid we are, the more the sensation of suffering will increase.

This does not mean that pain does not exist: it does exist, but the courage and strength to face it, to overcome it and to reduce it, also exist.

Pain is the vehicle of consciousness, as we have been taught. Is it wise to undervalue this school of life? Pain is not the main factor: the important thing is to become conscious and, once this happens, the pain will diminish and, on the other hand, the means to fight what gave rise to the suffering will appear.

Fear is like a blanket of fog that prevents us from seeing the world, or even ourselves. It indicates psychological weakness which, as we mentioned before, also becomes physical and mental weakness when it prevents us from moving and acting. And the more one remains motionless due to fear, the weaker one becomes, in the same way that a person who remains seated in a chair forever will eventually lose the use of their muscles.

Fear is a weakness that stunts our progress on the path to victory. By developing a healthy courage - which is not recklessness - a healthy confidence in oneself and in the teachings learned, and by keeping one's will firm by exercising it little by little every day, the traveller dissipates the fog surrounding him, his weakness, and is able to start walking again.

What can we do? Act

What, then, can we do with our fears?

A simple analysis shows us that, since fear is like a claw that immobilizes us, the only thing that can help us is action. We need to get out of the state of inertia with a spirit of risk and victory.

Against fear, action.

In action there is a vibration that enables us to emerge from every kind of inertia, from every kind of immobility. It is action that lifts us out of the heaviness of the rock, that frees us from the roots that cling to the earth. It is action that gives our higher feelings wings, that brings light to our ideas.

Walking is not only the action of the feet; it is above all the action of our hearts which feel and know what they have to do; it is the action of our minds, which understand what are the ideas that move us; it is the action of the spirit, which obliges us to keep returning eternally. It is the action that leads all of us in an immense spiral; we carve out a spiral path for ourselves and leave furrows behind us as we ascend in space and time. Difficult furrows, because there must be a space for each one, a time for each one and, at the same time, space and time for all of us who have planted a tree and not only take shelter in its shade, but also want to use it to climb up to heaven.

We need to pay attention to everything we do. There are mechanical, habitual actions that add nothing to our discernment or our evolution. They are just movements, the inevitable movements of a world in which everything vibrates, in which everything is in action. And although those movements, in the long term, lead towards constant improvement, it is not the same to give in to the unconscious slowness of the current of life as to work consciously with and for the laws of nature.

There are actions that keep us fixed in a single place, not in space, but in evolution. These are the mechanical and routine actions. Although it is true that we need many of them to live with a certain amount of ease and dedicate our mind to other occupations, too much mechanical action ends by making the mind stagnate. We know that walking, moving our tongue when speaking, typing, certain movements while driving a car and many other similar examples are habits that enable us to save time. But the convenience of the personality, which always tries to economize efforts in all senses, means that these more or less unconscious repetitions get transferred to other planes where the freshness of each moment is indispensable.

There are also actions which make us grow. These are the intelligent ones, those which we introduce into our lives in order to attain higher goals. They are the new experiences, the new steps we take in the conquest of our Self, the inner axis.

We should put our greatest interest and effort into the actions that make us grow. It is not enough to have reached a point of personal development; a philosopher is never satisfied with what he has but aspires to more and better, whenever he perceives higher and better goals. No one can assert: "Now I have arrived", or "I am fine as I am", because with that they are demonstrating a self-complacency which is no more than laziness and lack of willpower.

Among the actions that make us grow, decisiveness holds a prominent place. In order to grow, to progress, we have to decide to do so.

Decisiveness is not the misconceived initiative of doing many things, or new things, or anything which is out of the ordinary. Decisiveness is the inner power to put into practice the teachings received in order to become better, to master consecutive steps on the path of knowledge, to apply what so many teachers of humanity have pointed to as guidelines for attaining wisdom.

To grow, to evolve, are not empty words or, at most, abstract goals which we have no idea how to achieve. Anyone who thinks like that is precisely lacking in decisiveness and prefers to remain in the field of passive actions. To grow, to evolve, are active concepts which contain within them the range of experiences and advice of all those great beings who have preceded us on the path we are attempting to follow today.

Growth is an inescapable duty for all of us. However, it is essential to recognize the characteristics of growth, since all growth has to start from within. It is the root that makes the tree strong, not the number of leaves. We must not lose the memory of that root. The aims and principles, and the need to establish a chain of continuity, should be the ever-present cause in each of our actions.

The cause is our driving force. Actions are the response to the driving force. Our effects must be in accordance with our cause.

Decisiveness, knowing, wanting and being able to act in the appropriate way, according to the teachings and experiences, are the outcomes of many quality actions. They are some of the great keys to action.

It is always a good time to decide to be decisive.

The invisible barriers to action

Decisiveness is the power to set things in motion. And here we have one of the first and foremost barriers: to move from ideas to action.

What can we do with this barrier?

The first thing is to become aware of it, to accept that it exists, because it is impossible to overcome something that we deny or are unaware of.

It is not easy to explain what holds us back when we need to move into action. Why we become paralyzed when we are convinced of what we have to do, when we are supported by our own reason and motivated by our feelings.

The barrier, as such, is real. It is real because it does indeed hold us back. But it is made up of many illusions, some of them greater than others, although each of them, separately, would not withstand the force of the will. However, all those illusions become powerful when combined; they add up, and even multiply and are exponentially increased by being united. They are the many invisible barriers that build up the Great Barrier, the great obstacle on the path towards victory.

What are some of these illusions?

- Making our actions dependent on circumstances.

This translates more or less as: when everything is fine, when everything is in its place (or what I consider to be its place), when all the stars are aligned, when the weather has improved, when some of the problems I have at the moment have been solved, when the work on my house has been finished, when I have changed my job, when I have finished my studies... then I will be able to act without risks.

It goes without saying that such a combination of circumstances will never occur just as we want it to. Or what we want is so impossible that we present it in that way precisely in order to avoid having to act.

Every action has its time and its place and, although it is combined with many other circumstances, it is to a certain extent independent. If this were not so, we would never do anything.

Perhaps, if we were to make our actions non-dependent, we would become able to solve hundreds of adverse external circumstances.

- Making our actions dependent on other people.

This translates more or less as: what will people say? What will people think of me? Won't I lose people's affection and respect? Will people be able to understand, value or justify what I am going to do? And many other similar arguments which express the fear of not having the approval or love of others, of those close to us and those not so close to us.

However hard it may be to accept, the people who really love us will always try to understand us, whatever we may do, and especially if we do what we consider to be right and necessary. And the people who don't love us will carry on not loving us whatever we do. It is not by satisfying others that we will succeed in gaining their affection; a person who gives us their affection only when we do what they want will take that affection away from us at the slightest change of mood or attitude on our part.

I think that these two headings cover a large number of invisible barriers - of time, place, events, persons, feelings, the consent of others, unconfessed fears, hidden cowardice, hidden pride, lack of willpower, weakness when it comes to acting.

In this short summary, everyone will be able to find one or several of their deceptive barriers. So, it is for each of us to dare to break through our paper doors, which have the appearance of solid fortresses but are little more than an illusion. It is for each of us to dare to face our barrier made of clouds and begin to feel within us the unstoppable force of our willpower made reality.

Nothing is achieved without effort.

Effort

We all have a certain amount of energy available to us, generally much more than we think; but, as we don't make use of it, we imagine it to be small and limited.

That energy is valid for all planes, from the physical to the plane of will. It is easy to imagine a physical effort, even if it is not so easy to make it, but at least we know what kind of energy is involved. But it is not so easy to recognize effort, energy, on an emotional, mental, moral and spiritual level.

On the more subtle planes, effort is related to good spirits, to cheerfulness. Psychologically, it is the energy that allows us to keep our moods serene, stable, cheerful, to avoid negative and excessive emotions. We have to make an effort, we have to use a lot of energy to achieve that very special state of mind, but it is well worth it.

Mentally, energy is used to clarify all the ideas we learn, instead of moving in a nebulous world of complex ideas where nothing has defined contours. It is the energy needed to put all our ideas in order, harmoniously linking ideas with each other in the marvellous architecture of thought. We have to make an effort to transform the mind into a world of organised and valid forms, and of course that is worth the effort.

Seen in this light, effort is nothing more and nothing less than courage. It is that condition of the soul which, without giving in to irrational outbursts, takes intelligence as its guide and sets off in search of the best conquests: the conquest of oneself in order to place oneself at the service of humanity, in order to leave the world a little better than we found it. It is the moral and spiritual courage to overcome our limitations, without being afraid to discover the great source of potential that sleeps in the ignorance of our unknown inner world.

But effort has a secret that makes it continually lighter, more pleasant and more of a friend to the higher self: it is continuity, the perseverance that knows nothing of discouragement or stopping at the wrong time and place. When effort springs from our own flow of energy, when we discover that we are much stronger than we thought, when we accumulate courage and apply consistent perseverance, then effort is the strength of the human being who fights to attain victory. It is the energy that leads him to the goal, the energy that will surely bring him face to face with the calm countenance of wisdom.

Negligence

Negligence is a form of inaction. It never presents itself as such, but is always dressed up in a thousand excuses which help it to enter our domains.

Negligence feeds on our "moments of forgetfulness", which are in fact the desire not to remember those tedious, boring, difficult things, in short "what we don't want to do". That is why we forget, that is why we respond so often with the terrible refrain, “I forgot”, which means “I chose not to remember it”.

Negligence feeds on our procrastination: “I still have time, there’s still some time to go... I’ll do it tomorrow, I’ll see if I can find someone else to do it, there’s no rush...” These acts of procrastination are a kind of forgetfulness; the only difference is that instead of relegating these obligations to the subconscious, we relegate them in time. The excuses of perfectionism are not valid in this case either: “I will take more time because I want to do it really well.” If you never learn to do something - and you only learn by practising - it doesn’t matter whether you have more or less time. Let us not forget that we human beings have a strange weakness for “the pleasure of the last minute.”

Negligence feeds on things done half-heartedly, in order to get by, to do just enough (or even less) to ensure that our lack of efficiency won’t be too noticeable. Those things that are done half-heartedly are worse than those that are done badly: if we are to be an example to others, it will hardly be by producing work that is missing details, not properly finished and of dubious quality, and to cap it all by blaming others, or “difficult circumstances”, because it didn’t turn out well.

Negligence begins with a lack of sense of responsibility: if we don’t feel fully involved in what we are doing, if we don’t feel that it is a part of us, if we don’t see the impact of our carelessness, our actions become sloppy. It is as if we were doing a favour for an unknown person, for which in any case we won’t obtain anything.

Negligence stems from a false conception of time and our ability to manage time. It is to believe that we can do a lot in a short space of time, when in fact we do not need a lot or a little, but the right amount to do what we have to do according to our abilities. Everyone should learn to know themselves in this respect and not deceive themselves. To lie to ourselves, not to see ourselves as we are, is a form of negligence: the negligence of someone who runs away from their own reality and, therefore, from their possibility of self-improvement and growth.

Negligence is the opposite of diligence, and diligence is necessary to overcome fears and increase our knowledge of how to do things.

We have come here to learn, and in order to learn we have to go through the natural mistakes that allow us to apply the teachings of the great sages of humanity, which are nothing more and nothing less than the great corrections that wisdom offers us, so that we can become what we dream of becoming.

There is a great distance between acknowledging fears and having the courage to deal with them.

The fingers of fear are very long and very similar to one another, just like the fingers of a hand, which seem different but are ultimately all fingers.

Dreams die if we let them die, if we depend exclusively on external motivations to keep them alive: if there are people who keep our spirits up, we are in good spirits, if those people are not around, we have no more energy; if circumstances are favourable we feel encouraged, but if something goes slightly wrong, we fall apart. This is not how to live a dream, this is not how to express enthusiasm. In that way we will always be victims of the hands of fear.

Be a good traveller: don't be afraid of failure. No one can make you fail if you want to succeed. And you can succeed if you adopt the simple but powerful ethical and aesthetic principles that have been the basis of the highest civilizations. The long fingers of fear do not reach the summit of the pyramid.

Courage

We are at a major turning point in history.

The whole world is breaking at its hinges in many different places; and when the whole world is changing so much, when the world is moving so fast, when history is becoming like the wind, then we human beings must be alert and prepare ourselves. Because these are hard and difficult times, these are moments when history is accelerating, when it is changing from one situation to another, they are times that strip away masks, that remove all superficial veneers and falsehoods. These are times when we see things face to face, with the eyes of the soul. In these times, the soul is trying to breathe, to emerge from the depths of its darkness, of mud and matter, and that is why we are preparing for battle.

We are facing a great battle of giants: great black giants, and great white giants. The black giants represent everything that appears to be, everything that "is not" and wants to occupy a place in the world that does not correspond to it. The white giants represent what is, because it always has been and always will be; they represent something that is claiming its throne, that wants to be among human beings and wants to be able to look at the gods again.

It takes a lot of strength to try to know oneself in such times as we are living in. It takes a lot of strength to love wisdom, a lot of strength to keep walking and to call ourselves seekers of knowledge, and to say it aloud. A lot of strength to "honour every truth by use", as H.P. Blavatsky used to say.

These are hard times... times of trial, when we will have to become white giants, to rise to the height of those who have always pointed out the path of truth. The task of the white giants is to improve the world and leave a trail of noble actions, to fight to create space for higher sentiments such as fraternity, harmonious coexistence, love. It is time to bring not reasons, but ideas; and not only ideas, but ideals; and not only ideals, but will.

What is courage?

"We will call an individual courageous when that part in which the spirited nature resides follows without hesitation, in pleasure and in pain, the commands of reason as to what is or is not to be feared" (Plato).

This is the courage that most interests us: the courage which, fired with a love for justice and a healthy spiritedness, obeys intelligence in order to counteract internal and external threats. It is a harmonious combination of the most noble sentiments and the knowledge that is most in accordance with wisdom.

If instinct predominates, courage becomes recklessness and leads individuals to take on dangers beyond their reach, or which only satisfy their vanity; and in that case they will be closer to failure than to victory. Whereas if only cold reflection predominates, it is possible that the person will not be courageous, but merely indifferent. As we well know, in our world of dualities, such indifference is not exactly a virtue: someone who does not know fear, who has never been afraid, cannot distinguish what courage, or the capacity to overcome fear, is.

Thus, we come to the conclusion that courage is an elevated sentiment, and it is elevated precisely because it expresses itself when it becomes the ally of intelligence. When courage - the 'spirited nature' of Plato - acts in favour of the instincts, it is not true courage, but an unleashed instinctive force which takes no account of good or evil, large or small, and therefore, cannot achieve victories, only uncontrolled outbursts.

If we research the origin of the word *courage* we will find that it is very similar to the idea of bravery and that spirited part of the soul mentioned by Plato.

This term, which is used in several languages and written and pronounced in similar ways, comes from the Latin *cor* - 'heart' - and *agere* - 'to act'.

To sum up: *coragere* is to act with the heart. It is another root that links to the word 'concord', because the heart that makes us act with courage does not arise from coarse and fleeting emotions, but from the great heart, the heart which can resonate with the harmony of the universe, which knows how to stand together with other hearts. Our dearly beloved concord, then, joins hands with valour and becomes courage.

From this we could deduce that the soul has an intelligent, reasoning part and a desiring part subject to the instincts. In between there is a variable element: if it inclines towards the lustful passions, it is anger; if, on the other hand, it rises towards intelligence, it becomes courage, valour, the indispensable action with the heart which distinguishes the human being.

Self-conquest does not need anger, but it does need courage. The first path will lead us towards certain slavery; the second, towards a developed freedom of the conscious Self. Once again, the choice lies within us.

Anger is a strong emotion, a blinding passion that makes us lose the little control we have over the personality as a whole. It does not listen to reason, but is buffeted by the winds of the psyche that drag it from side to side with uncontrollable force. Under the effects of anger, one can utter the most absurd, most hurtful words, that have nothing to do with what the person's soul really feels; anger dilutes one's own identity and presents a deformed and violent mask. The features of the face change, the gaze becomes distorted, it is difficult to recognize the person who is under the effects of such a powerful demon.

In short, anger makes us manipulable slaves. The loss of self-control leaves us under the control of those who know how to take advantage of this situation for their own benefit. The soul of the angry person is in the hands of others...

It is good to master anger and even better to replace it with courage. Courage awakens the true heart, the true human soul. Courage is to have the strength to see things as they are, to moderate the emotions, to listen, to interpret ideas, to choose what is valid, to discard what is useless, to act with justice.

The heart

How else can a human being act if not with the heart? The heart represents the mid-point in our sevenfold constitution: not the emotional or feeling psyche, but the mind with emotions or emotion with thoughts; it is the central level that seeks equilibrium between a lower part - of which we already have experience - and a higher part which is yet to be attained.

The heart is the axis, the point of stability if we know how to combine the requirements of the body with the spiritual realities. But that heart often becomes disturbed and moves towards one of the two pans of the scales. That is why we need courage: to act with the heart, in a constant search for harmony and equilibrium.

Through courage we will reach higher, achieve a true equilibrium, which is not to provide equal satisfaction to the body and the spirit. On the contrary, equilibrium is achieved when the spirit, as light as a feather, has the same value and weight as the heart filled with actions, correct or incorrect, accurate or inaccurate, wise or ignorant... Or the other way around: when the heart, as a result of acting for the good and for justice, becomes as light as a feather.

Let us now look at different ways of acting with the heart:

- Action in which emotion predominates, even if it inclines toward noble causes. But emotion alone is unstable and can lose sight of its objectives at any time, changing its course, ceasing to act or acting in an exaggerated way, to the point of recklessness.

- Action in which the prudent heart predominates, in which case the emotion is less irrational and more human. Under an apparent coldness - which is serenity - the most difficult enterprises in the most dangerous places are undertaken without fear or doubt - which is militancy. Perhaps the doubts and fears are hidden in the folds of consciousness, but courage has the necessary power to refute the doubts and soothe the fears.

- Bravery is the practice of courage, of intelligent action done with heart. It is the great militancy.

Let us remember that as human beings we will be judged by our heart, by our valour or courage. Ancient Egyptian rituals represented that moment by the scene of the "weighing" of the heart of the deceased, in which it was shown that individual karma affects the actions of the Self, in other words, those actions that have been dictated by the Individual, those good or bad actions that have been done "from the heart". In this way, individual karma measures our degree of individualization, which is equivalent to our heart still subject to action and, therefore, to reaction. That is what we should achieve in life: to follow the heart and make the wilful heart follow prudent wisdom.

The ancient Egyptians of the early dynasties used to say: *"The heart is the source of all knowledge and the tongue repeats what the heart has thought."*

Shields

Courage protects, anger destroys. There are shields that protect and shields that destroy. This is a very interesting aspect of the heroic path.

Without leaving aside the reading of edifying adventures in which we learned to recognize great heroes protected by extraordinary shields, we know that each person possesses their own shield made of subtle materials that come from their own vehicles of expression.

Out of elements projected by our physical, energetic, emotional and mental bodies, and even by the higher bodies of our spiritual Self, a shield is formed. It primarily covers the personality, that part of ourselves that moves and shows itself in concrete, manifested life.

If the shield is properly constructed, it provides an effective defence against aggression from both within and without.

The shield truly arises out of our internal energies: it is the result of our best thoughts, our best emotions, the healthiest aspects of our energies and actions. It is the sum of our virtues and powers, our experiences and achievements, our affirmations and growth, our love and generosity, our sacrifice and willpower, our idealism and purity. With those characteristics, the shield will prevent our defects and negative drives, which also come from within, from destroying our well-established personality. At the same time, all the harmful elements that reach us from outside strike this luminous shield and bounce off it, enabling us to maintain a remarkable equilibrium.

Simply put, the shield generates something like an "atmosphere" around us, which only allows the best of what arises inside us and the best of what comes from the outside to pass through it. It filters the energies and continues to nourish and strengthen itself with all the positive aspects that are in tune with its protective nature.

But we should also be aware that there are destructive shields and that we ourselves are responsible for this negative condition.

Sometimes our shields turn against us and stop working in the way they were intended, becoming weapons that wound us instead. How could this point have been reached?

DUE TO WEAR AND TEAR. A shield needs care, like all things; if it is neglected, if it is not properly nourished, if it is not cleaned and polished as if it were made of bright metal or wood and leather, if its toughness is not checked from time to time, it loses its strength and begins to display cracks which, in a short time, will turn into holes. Through these, all the corrosive acids from which we had been protected until then will be able to enter.

DUE TO A REVERSAL OF VALUES. If great moral and spiritual driving forces were needed to construct the shield, it is evident that the lack of such driving forces or the appearance of an opposing energy, will turn it against us. We have to beware of the passivity that disturbs and prevents our continuous development. We should watch over our so-called failures, which are no more than trials that life presents us with in its effort to educate, and turn them into enriching experiences rather than justifications for giving up or abandoning the heroic path that has allowed us to be reborn. We should fight selfishness, rash passions that take the place of sober will, obsessive depressions that are not looking for solutions but pity from others, aggression and oversensitivity. We cannot walk "naked" through the world, without that shield which is a part of ourselves and an indispensable tool for evolution.

There is no point dreaming of past or imaginary heroes, or contenting ourselves with the sterile imagination of those who believe they are living through the actions of others. Those who were and are true heroes were able to construct and maintain their shields, and not just the gleaming ones we see in the images of war.

We too have the individual and inalienable task of making our shields, those weapons that will help us to emerge triumphant from the difficult trials of existence.

Life teaches us, but life is a battle in the broadest and most philosophical sense of the word: there is a constant warfare between forces of an opposing nature which compel us to choose, to make decisions, to make our way forward without falling into hidden traps. Therefore, we must be well protected in order to overcome our trials, even if sometimes we will be left with the honourable memory of a blow and a dent in our shield. Those are our distinctions.

Limits and limitations

If we seriously want to make progress on the path to victory, we need to be able to distinguish between natural limits and artificial limitations.

Natural limits are those that are part of our human condition; it is evident that we have qualities and possibilities that are higher than those of stones, plants and animals, but we can also see that, from the evolutionary level where we are now, we cannot become one with the mystery of life that lies hidden in the stars. Nevertheless, there is an underlying aspiration of the soul which impels us towards the heights and urges us to reach the point that other great souls have reached, if not as stars, at least - some day - as wiser and more fulfilled human beings.

That is why natural limits are only signposts on the path, milestones that give us some indication of how far we have travelled. They are never unsurmountable barriers; rather, they are calls from the higher planes that encourage us to keep going forward.

It is not those natural limits, however, that hinder our progress. The difficulty arises, in most cases, from the limitations we impose upon ourselves. Whether due to a lack of knowledge, a weak and undisciplined personality, inner laziness, indecisiveness, or even pride, there are people who limit themselves by closing themselves off to any possibility of taking new steps on the path.

Lack of knowledge is easy to solve because we all have access to sources of learning that can help us in this difficulty. The problem is when we have the knowledge but lack even the slightest willpower to apply it in an appropriate and progressive way. A weak personality can be strengthened in the same way as a muscle can be strengthened or the number of red corpuscles in the blood can be increased through medication when necessary; to achieve it, all we have to do is carry out a number of practical daily exercises that have been designed for that purpose. Laziness and indecisiveness are limitations that indicate, once again, a lack of will; the lazy person knows they could make progress, but it is easier to stay where they are and complain - they can do that, at least - about the difficulties that life presents them with, instead of recognizing that it is they themselves who have blocked their own way. The indecisive person prefers to spend their existence hesitating between various possibilities and keeping their mind and emotions entertained in an apparent search for truth that is no more than a game to avoid making decisions. The most difficult case is that of the proud person who believes they have achieved the greatest truth for themselves and considers, for that very reason, that they have nothing more to do; their limitation is unconscious or is disguised as a sense of having overcome everything.

The first thing we need to do is to acknowledge limitations and give them their true value.

What are limitations? Iron bars or elastic bands? Are they traps of destiny or trials to make us stronger? It all depends on our mental attitude and our moral integrity.

If our mental attitude is positive, we will know that limitations, which are the result of our inexperience, are elastic bands, sometimes a little hard to move, but elastic nevertheless. By persevering in the appropriate action and direction, we will eventually overcome the resistance offered by these bands and use their elasticity to expand our horizons.

If our mental attitude is positive, we will know that every apparent limitation is no more than a trial to determine to what extent we are capable of earning our place and continuing to rise upwards in the conquest of ourselves. Instead of putting the blame on destiny, we should be grateful for the opportunities it offers us to prove ourselves and increase our confidence in our inner strength.

Moral integrity depends on the outcome of our struggle against fear. Fear can establish itself in any of our bodies and thus become one of the greatest limitations we can face. Fear can be physical and then it will hinder action; if it is emotional, it will raise unsurmountable walls where none exist or take the shape of monsters that will entangle our feet; if it is mental, it will make everything seem difficult, uncertain and incomprehensible, making it impossible to adopt the positive mental attitude mentioned above.

We insist: limitations are a product of ourselves and, out of all of them, the hardest to overcome is fear.

Then, in the second place, once we have recognized the nature of limitations, we have to begin by demolishing those artificial boundaries, opening doors and windows, discovering new horizons and going fearlessly towards them. The battle against limitations begins by accepting that it is the human being who imposes them and, consequently, that the same human being who put them in place can also remove them.

We must work with the natural limits and even try to go beyond them, but we should never resign ourselves to remaining in the same place or in the same inner state. If we add to these natural limits, which are like milestones on the path, the limitations that arise from human incompetence, the only thing we will achieve is to become eternal complainers, people who demand pity from others without making the least effort to escape from the small prison they have built around themselves.

Effort is a law of life and is the antidote to limits and limitations.

Winning the battle or accepting defeat

An ancient Tibetan teaching aimed at disciples says: "Look for the warrior and let him fight in you."

Once again, the warrior we already know from the Bhagavad Gita - Arjuna - reappears on the path of inner growth. He is, of course, no ordinary warrior and his battles are not fought against other human beings, or with conventional weapons. The warrior is Arjuna's own Self, subjected to the many trials that life sets before him. His fight is an inner and solitary battle: his task is to make way for the powerful force of the will, which will enable him to transform himself in a positive way.

It is to the inner warrior, to the one who fights within each one of us, that these words are addressed. It is the seeker, young or adult, beginner or veteran on the philosophical path - the warrior, in a word - whom we are inviting to this reflection.

Every battle leads to two possible outcomes: victory or defeat. Those battles that are left half-finished, inconclusive, are actually already lost, as they will have to be repeated until a clear result has been obtained. And on the basis of that result we can decide on the steps to be taken in the future.

What does it mean to win? Of course, we are referring here to just a single battle, rather than an entire war. To win a battle is to gain ground within ourselves, to reduce a weakness, a bad habit, to try to understand an idea, to begin to overcome comfort and laziness, both physical and mental, and to discover our own virtues. It is, in short, the beginning of many conquests that will be finally completed later on, when we can state with certainty that the individual has won the war.

To win in the first place means simply to begin the battle, but to begin it in reality, not in our fantasy. If the meaning and purpose of the battle begins to dawn in our consciousness, if we begin to perceive the existence of that mystical and living warrior, who has to map out his path with his own courage, this will be a first step, a beginning. This will be a first victory, because to win does not imply to overcome all defects or to acquire every possible virtue. To win one must begin by achieving small victories that will increasingly strengthen the will, until it becomes the most powerful of tools.

To win is to know that we are not perfect; that is exactly why we are warriors and are fighting a battle. One who is perfect has attained absolute peace. We, on the other hand, are perfectible; in other words, it is in our power to achieve what we have proposed to accomplish, step by step, without being held back by any obstacle.

What does it mean, on the other hand, to accept defeat?

We should not think of it only in terms of that well-known expression of Arjuna: "I will not fight". This attitude would evidently lead to inevitable defeat.

To accept defeat is sometimes far more subtle, such as using justifications that lead us to abandon the battle, not through any fault of our own, of course, but because the circumstances are so difficult that there is no other option.

Some of the most common justifications can even look like a form of good intention. They are the ones that are expressed as "I don't measure up", "I'm not at the level of what is expected of me", and therefore I give up my place to make way for others who are better and more capable.

This apparent generosity is nothing more than weakness.

How does a person know that they are not at the level that is expected of them? Simply because they do in fact know the stature or level that is required, and because rather than trying to achieve it, they assume it isn't possible. And a person who argues that they have already made many efforts and have still not managed to make any progress has in fact moved only in their fantasy, has made feeble, misdirected, discontinuous attempts without any clear aim. Let us try approaching it from the opposite angle: let us clarify the aims, that is to say, what is expected of us as human beings in evolution; let us leave aside imagination and enter into action, at least into small daily actions; let us insist on continuity, with the support of perseverance, and we will find that we are moving imperceptibly towards the goal.

To accept defeat is to abandon the battle before we have even started. It is to judge ourselves without knowing how to judge: to evaluate our own strengths without listening to how others evaluate our capacities. It is to decide to run away from responsibilities instead of accepting them. It is to hide away from difficulties. It is to evade the struggle out of fear of losing the little comfort that is provided to us by "remaining as we are." It is fear of the battle and fear of success. That is why it can be called accepting defeat. Not in the face of any enemy in particular: rather, it is allowing oneself to be defeated by one's own fragility. And there is nothing harder for the consciousness than having to acknowledge, at some point, that: I wanted to, but I couldn't.

We end where we began: let the warrior within you arise and dare to fight. You may receive some wounds due to the natural confrontation with the trials you will have to face. But they are not mortal wounds; they are just scratches that heal quickly. The aim is to strengthen the inner being, to make room for the spirit which, up to now, has been subjected to the passions of the senses; to open the eyes to ancient truths clothed in new words, to awaken the philosopher who knows how to search for wisdom, and not just search for it, but find it too.

He who finds, wins.

To survive is not only about staying alive; it is about not giving in, not falling, not surrendering. To survive is to preserve the energy of life. And that is something we have definitely learned.

And while we are fighting and winning, we are exercising our moral strengths, we are giving them form and power, we are becoming heroically greater.

To fight against the psychological comfort which calls us to the sleep of forgetfulness, to the desire to let ourselves be carried along by the current of a vegetative life, is to stand in front of the claws of the enemy with a spirit of victory.

To fight against the comfort of imagining life instead of living it is equivalent to facing the enemy.

To fight against the cowardice of leaving in the hands of others what we can do ourselves is also to face the enemy.

To fight against the ignoble attitude of demanding instead of giving is to be able to look the enemy in the face.

To fight against ignorance, by sowing seeds of deep and simple knowledge that can be applied in life, is to undermine the enemy.

To fight against injustice by being just, in spite of our inner struggles, is to destroy the enemy.

Victory

"O Powerful Victory, by men desired...
Thee I invoke... For thou rulest all things, Victory divine!
And glorious strife, and joyful shouts are thine..."
(Orphic Hymn)

What is victory?

Seen objectively, victory is just a deity governing success in battle. Or the advantage gained in a contest.

We believe, however, that the cultures of antiquity were more interested in seeing the inner, subjective value of things than their superficial appearances. For them, appearances were no more than the final visible and objective manifestation of profound ideas.

Our task, therefore, is to recover the meaning of war, the meaning of success and the meaning of victory, not as an advantage but as the overcoming of oneself.

Weaknesses come disguised under the mask of comfort, and that makes them attractive. On the other hand, the positive potentials are not often activated; in most cases they remain latent, hidden, as if they did not exist. An effort of intelligence is required to discover them, and an effort of will to set them in motion. Although their discovery and activation may seem to make us weaker, they are nevertheless the strongest aspect of our being.

We would like victory to come of its own accord, without any risk on our part. We think of it as something owed to us by destiny, without realising that we are the ones who are in debt: because we were unable to see or take advantage of the opportunities, and because we mistook the best chances to grow for causes of passive suffering.

Success is an objective fact.

Victory is a state of the soul. It is the inner joy that wells up in the face of success when we have put all our efforts into it.

Success, on its own, may satisfy vanity.

But the sentiment of victory ennobles the soul.

Success can be the culmination of different types of goals, which in most cases are relative and transitory.

Victory provides stable and lasting conquests in the inner human being, which enable us to keep moving forward on the path of further achievements.

VICTORY ACHIEVED WITH COMPLETE CONFIDENCE

Although all forms of victory can often look like distant and inaccessible goals, this one, which is the fruit of self-confidence, becomes the summit of victory.

This victory is not only about achieving success and experiencing a sense of fullness of the soul, but also represents the victory of the human being who has conquered himself. This is why he is sure of himself and of what he needs to do to achieve his objectives.

Complete confidence is also a state of the soul, like victory.

It bears no relation to the vanity, arrogance or pride of those who feel great without having accumulated any merit apart from always seeing themselves in a good light. That is not confidence, but a very basic kind of self-satisfaction. Complete confidence is the result of many trials, mistakes and corrections, a great deal of patience, many sufferings and the attitude of picking oneself up after every fall. It is the expression of continuous work over time. It is the knowledge obtained after many investigations and many inquiries into the innermost parts of the soul, resulting in the consolidation of what we have learned, as we recognize the difference between what we were previously unaware of and what we now understand.

To sum up, complete confidence is the result of an intelligent effort. It is to have a clear goal in front of us and to walk straight towards it, without getting side-tracked or stopping. It is not a gift; it is something we acquire, it is a sign of spiritual maturity.

Complete confidence is such an elevated state that it is sometimes confused with inspiration. Or perhaps they are one and the same? What geniuses and mystics achieve by elevating the soul, those who master themselves achieve by effort: both succeed in glimpsing the same intuitions.

What, then, does the victory of one who has achieved self-confidence consist of?

In achieving success by superabundance, because that person has a surplus of resources, because they have practised so much and are so familiar with what they have to do that their whole being walks calmly towards the goal.

Have you never experienced a taste of this particular aspect of victory?

Almost certainly you have.

When you have prepared yourself to the best of your ability for an exam, a test or an interview, you will have noticed that the questions didn't unsettle you; on the contrary, you were happy to be able to give the right answers and to speak with complete confidence.

When you have done a job conscientiously, paying attention to every detail, you will have felt fully confident about your work and happy to have completed it.

When you have prepared well for a lecture or a more informal talk, and were fully familiar with all your ideas and the order in which you were going to present them, you will have enjoyed speaking, enjoyed the company of the audience, felt a connection with the people listening to you and generated an atmosphere of happiness and victory around you.

And a similar thing will have happened to you when giving a class, or explaining your thoughts and arguments, when the knowledge was not just from a book or some course notes, but it was your own soul that was expressing itself with complete confidence, with complete freedom, with complete happiness.

Now, too, you have an excellent opportunity: if you feel the complete certainty of being a philosopher, you will achieve a victory with complete confidence. You will have to work hard - no one will take that part of the path away from you. But when you arrive, you will be able to handle yourself and your circumstances with the same skill as a musician handles his instrument: he speaks to it, and he enters into a dialogue with people and with life. You will be a victorious philosopher. You will have your well-deserved crown of laurels and you will be confident that you can wear it with dignity.

The foundations of victory

There are victories that are won with COURAGE AND SPEED.

On previous occasions we have already referred to courage as a highly positive characteristic of the soul. Following Plato, we understand COURAGE OR BRAVERY to be the outcome of the soul that rises above the urges of desire and takes intelligence for its guide.

Hence, courage, in turn, contains many other values, including the ability to choose, to be decisive, to overcome impulses, to reflect with intelligence and, above all, to act. Still today, courage has the meaning of strength, power, vigour, resolution, fearlessness. And also, being healthy.

The STRENGTH we are interested in is not limited to the physical body. It is strength in a broader sense, which allows us to use our feelings and our ideas in a useful and effective way, for ourselves and for others. It is the strength of an inner column that supports the whole human structure.

POWER is the inner feeling of confidence that leads us to act in all fields of life; it helps us to correct ourselves when we make a mistake and to continue moving forward once we have corrected our mistakes. Power is not to depend on external factors, on the continual need to be admired and applauded by others; it is to believe in our own educated and developed consciousness.

VIGOUR is energy. If courage is to be real, it requires a lot of energy in all respects. Because true courage is not the impulse arising from a special moment, but the courage that lasts a lifetime. It is a constant action.

RESOLUTION is the ability to solve problems and the consequent actions we take in order to achieve a good end result.

FEARLESSNESS is daring, that is to say, the courage to face difficulties. It is courage in the face of danger or, even better, the courage to make the danger retreat.

BEING HEALTHY is to enjoy good health. And, as we said of strength, it is a health that goes beyond the physical body, because a healthy balance requires the emotions and the mind to be in good condition as well. All of this requires courage, whether to stay healthy or to regain health. Someone who is not healthy will not be able to face up to the battles of life, let alone emerge victorious.

This is why victory goes hand in hand with courage. Heroes are courageous.

To be a philosopher is a courageous way of living life, in which all efforts are coordinated so that thoughts and feelings are reflected in actions.

Victory and philosophy are good companions.

And finally, we come to the other factor that must be combined with courage: SPEED.

The philosopher does not think of speed as a hasty action, which does not reflect on the means to be used or the consequences that may arise from it.

Speed is to act in harmony with time, following its vital rhythm. In nature nothing stops, everything follows a continuous course and aims for a specific end, whether we know it or not. That is the virtue which has to be conquered in order to achieve victory.

If actions are delayed, if they are slowly executed, the energy of courage becomes like stagnant water… Only speed imprints on actions the necessary vigour that enables them to achieve their goal in time. Solutions that are not on time are not solutions… We want speed because, as we have seen, it helps us not to be held back by obstacles, to follow the rhythm of nature with the same tenacity as a river flows towards the sea, and to eliminate slowness, the inertia caused by the weight of what is crude and material.

Now we see it more clearly: if there is still a victory we have yet to win, if there is something we really want to see achieved, we have to take hold of the rung of courage and speed.

This will be our first, small and humble crown of laurels.

FORCEFULNESS, like so many other concepts, has lost its real meaning and has been reduced to a vulgar kind of violence, to the fury of a person who is virtually unable to restrain their passions.

But the victorious warrior knows the other side of forcefulness, in which force, energy, speed, the severe grandeur of the soul and fieriness are combined.

We want the forcefulness of one who lives in peace with his soul and takes from it the greatness that inspires his whole existence.

The forceful hero is firm with himself, bold in his undertakings and great and generous in his actions.

Forcefulness is fiery because it carries within itself the heat and light of fire. Without the ardent flame that illuminates the soul, life lacks meaning, and human beings lack the drive to accomplish their aims.

DETERMINATION is the strength to push against false doors, imaginary walls, giants that are only windmills... It is the constant effort to go forward; it is the persistence that doesn't give in to problems but, on the contrary, confidently looks for solutions.

We are about to climb up to a second rung. We know that many struggles await us before we can achieve victory, but we also know that forcefulness illuminates us and determination urges us on.

The moral struggle

The true philosopher should think of his struggle as a moral battle.

The field of morality includes all those latent powers that are trying to emerge but are unable to do so, because they need our decisive and willing support. Morality is the sum of all our virtues, the combination of all our powers, active and latent; it is the armour and the weapons with which we enter the battle of life, from which we want to emerge victorious.

Morality, then, is the union of our physical, energetic, emotional, intellectual and spiritual potentials in their positive aspects.

Ours is a moral struggle to achieve the conquest of our human values. The effort and struggle that precede any victory, whether great or small, are especially evident on the innermost planes of the personality.

There is no doubt that many efforts require the active participation of the body and the energy. But the root of that physical effort is always to be found in the things we know or the things we want; the forces of wanting and knowing are powerful motivations.

It is clear that the most fearsome struggles take place in the emotions and the mind. Bodies undergo great pain when they suffer; but it is not comparable to the intensity of pain in the subtle bodies, for which there is no quick and easy remedy.

Calm is expressed as serenity, as peace.

Many brave fighters know how important it is to remain calm in the midst of battle.

When the goal has not yet been reached, when we are still following uncertain paths with many byways and hidden traps, it is not advisable to lose control of ourselves or of the external circumstances.

The destabilizing element of aimless emotions, confused ideas and actions without continuity is the enemy that stands in the way of victory.

It is at these times that we are most in need of self-control. We have to know how to moderate the passions, clarify our ideas; we have to measure the movements of the body; we have to connect our actions. Everything must have an aim and, to ensure that the aim does not disappear from view, we need serenity.

Serenity does not imply insensitivity. It makes room for the best sentiments and enjoys them as long as they are expressed within ethical and aesthetic channels. It enables us to work with the best ideas because there is space, there is light and there is time to understand and develop them.

Serenity is a state of the soul which is very close to victory, even if it is not the great victory.

As regards peace, it was honoured on ancient altars as the deity that followed in the wake of victory. Victory gives rise to peace.

Our peace, for now, will be achieved by controlling our opposites. Calm victory, like all victories, cannot avoid inner struggles.

WE NEED TO KNOW THE TRUE NATURE OF SACRIFICE.

Sacrifice is not about pain, but about courageously exercised willpower.

Without looking very far, there is one well known explanation: sacrifice as self-denial, as the ability to put one's own desires aside and place oneself at the service of others. But in addition to self-denial we have the concept of sacrifice as *sacrum officium*, a sacred duty, a sacred action or offering. Altars, now and at all times, are those places where there is an opportunity for worthy and useful work. Sacrifice as a sacred offering is about creating more space in the soul.

The sacrifice that leads to victory has a lot to do with purification: leaving behind the residues and rubbish that obstruct the personality; it is impossible to move forward if our feet are stuck in the mud. It has a lot to do with generosity: possessing in order to give; only one who possesses can give and only one who is capable of giving possesses. It has a lot to do with mysticism: seeing what is hidden behind the appearances, perceiving the laws of nature in every action, understanding the purpose that moves the universe and all living beings.

This is the victory we must achieve. The victory that rises up like fire after the dross has been burnt. The ever-burning fire on the altars has a base of wood, a fuel that sets it alight and a star that attracts it.

Obstacles to overcome

Cunning is defined as the ability to deceive or to avoid being deceived. We can see, then, that it is not a defect in itself, although it might be if we spent our time deceiving others. On the other hand, it is a virtue if it is correctly applied. We are not interested in deceiving others, because no worthwhile victory can be sustained on the basis of lying and cheating. But we can and must avoid being deceived. This is where the virtue of cunning comes into play, a virtue which we so rarely apply.

The advantage of the virtues lies in their ability to elevate human beings towards their spiritual nature. Their disadvantage lies in the naïvety of the reasoning process of human beings and the lack of skill in the way they act, due to their own inexperience when they forget the voice of their teachers.

And what about defects?

They are older and more cunning. They retain all the experience of stones, plants and animals and overwhelm the human being with the weight of all that knowledge. The aim of defects is to prevent evolutionary progress, not out of any particular malice, but in order to keep things as they are. They are the defenders of the status quo, of what is already established, of routine, comfort, of thoughtless, impetuous and unreflecting action. They are opposed to any awakening of the latent powers because they know that it would lead to the end of their dominion.

Let us be always attentive, always ready for action, and when the defects allow themselves to be lulled to sleep by the certainty that we are already trapped, let us take a leap forward and pass through the illusory barriers they have set up in front of us.

Let us not argue with them, because in that sophistic battle we will always end up losing. Let us discover, on the other hand, the secret of action, which is motivated by higher feelings and intelligent goals, but does not waste time in useless discussions.

There is nothing better than to give battle when the enemy is not paying attention. This is cunning, rather than lying: it is not lying because the enemy knows that we are at war; it is not dishonour because the enemy also takes advantage of our weaknesses.

This is a victory obtained by taking a leap forward, taking advantage of the enemy's weak points to do so. It is interesting to try this out because, amongst other things, it will help us to discover many unusual aspects of our own latent powers.

There will always be difficulties, because there is no victory without a struggle. But we have to know how to distinguish between the real difficulties and the fantasies generated by fear.

Fear is dark and creates the same darkness inside and around us. We are unable to see within or discern what is going on outside.

We are in the middle of the night. The darkness rises up, all-enveloping, and hides all traces of victory.

We must learn, then, to be victorious in the night.

Let us begin by overcoming fear.

Fear is the trial. The goal is victory.

If we give in to circumstances, life loses all meaning and we lose sight of the future.

No one will shine a light in the darkness unless we do so ourselves. Let us learn not to expect solutions to come from outside.

If there are sources of light somewhere outside, it means that in some forgotten corner within us, there is light as well. We are not special beings in the world: there is the same in us as there is in the universe: light and darkness; and we have sufficient energies to generate both of them. Light a torch of hope for tomorrow, and even more, for today.

The great objective

If we want to make victory an integral part of ourselves and incorporate a few victories into our lives, we need to keep our feet on the ground, even if the soul rises up to heaven.

What do I want to do with my life? That is an essential question. And if we don't have a clear idea about that, what victories can we expect to achieve?

Once we have established where we want to go, there is still something equally important to do: to map out the route. It is not enough to gaze up to heaven; we have to build a ladder to get there.

This is where the small-great objectives come into play, the daily victories which, when added together and exponentially multiplied, will enable us to reach the desired goal.

And, finally, a recommendation to crown all others: we need to keep achieving those small daily victories and protect them as if they were the most precious treasures. They are the rungs by which, one by one, we will reach victory.

Epilogue

The hero is a doer of deeds; day by day he goes beyond his own possibilities, finding ways to increase and multiply them.

The hero is a conqueror. And the greatest of his conquests begins with himself, with the passing of tremendous trials that are always related to his duty, to his duty to be.

Until the hero finds himself, until he discovers his own inner powers, he will not be able to defeat his enemies or gain access to glory.

But for us there are no crowns of glory, because we have not reached the goal. There are no crowns of glory for us because we have not performed great deeds or obtained stable, lasting conquests.

All of us, whether victorious or not, have to start again.

We have found that, even when successes are real and objective, they are not as stable as we had imagined them to be. Of course we have achieved some successes, but we have also seen that we have to watch over them unceasingly if we are not to lose the ground we have won. If success is to be lasting, it must be accompanied by an alert and active attention.

To start again does not mean to repeat the same mistakes, but to continue without respite even when we have achieved a new level. It is not about imagining absolute successes, but recognizing that we still have a long way to go.

Victory is the apex of the pyramid, the golden summit which boldly enters the light of the sun. Our task, for now, is to follow in its footsteps, climbing up the different sides of the pyramid, step by step, consolidating each step, but without letting our feet become stuck at each place by looking for an undeserved rest.

OUR VICTORY IS TO START AGAIN.

IO TRIUMPHE[1]

1 A shout that was heard at the celebration of triumphs in Roman times.

Afterword

Through her elegant and profound use of language, Delia Steinberg has offered us the possibility of understanding life as an exciting adventure in search of the shining goal of victory.

For the author, who has dedicated most of her life to studying, living and transmitting the timeless philosophy that is to be found in the different cultures and civilisations of the world, victory is a state of consciousness which we all have the right to attain. If we can achieve it, we gain access to a source of energy that enables us to keep walking, day by day and step by step, along the long path of life.

It does not look like an easy task. But nor is it something so difficult or complicated that it is not even worth attempting.

Progress will largely depend on the confidence we have in our own powers, in our ability to learn, which must be gradually developed on each stretch of the path; on the skill of being able to take advantage of opportunities and enrich the soul through our encounters with other travellers who are walking in the same direction. Because no one is alone.

Many are the wise men and women who have preceded us on the path of wisdom, and their footsteps remain visible for those who want to see them, in spite of all the time that has passed. For the same reason, each of the steps we take will become a point of reference for other daring philosophers who undertake the adventure of self-conquest.

Delia Steinberg has made available to the reader her vast experience in this respect. Every idea, every image, even - dare I say? - each phrase, represents a real treasure of knowledge, especially for those who never give in to adversity.

If you are one of them or you want to become one, if you believe that life can have some meaning, if your heart harbours the firm intention to get up again as you shake the dust from the inevitable fall, if you don't want to give in to fears and difficulties, this little book will have been like a fresh wind which brings order to the mind and warms the heart. In it there are keys that enable us to come closer to victory over ourselves. Each battle fought will become a leaf in the well-deserved crown of laurels that will rest on our consciousness.

It only remains for me to express my profound gratitude to Delia Steinberg, my teacher on the path of perennial philosophy, for the unconditional love she has for her work of helping the thousands of students who follow her teachings throughout the world to learn. Her educational method is simple, and is as old as the natural human inclination to come closer to the wisdom that exists in all things and all beings: teaching by example. A daily example of effort and self-improvement, of joy and conviction.

I hope that these writings can be put to good use. They are the fruit of many experiences, of countless struggles against the superfluous, of inevitable advances and setbacks over time. They are the result of will, love and intelligence.

Carlos Adelantado

Delia Steinberg Guzmán

Delia Steinberg Guzmán was born in Buenos Aires (Argentina) on 7th January 1943.

In 1972, she moved to Madrid (Spain) and was granted Spanish nationality in 1975.

She has a degree in Philosophy from the University of Buenos Aires and graduated from the National Conservatory of Music in Buenos Aires as a Teacher of Piano and Composition. In 1982, she founded the piano competition which, since 2008, has been known in the musical world as the Delia Steinberg International Piano Competition. The competition is a member of the Alink-Argerich Foundation.

From 1972 to 1991 she was the Director of New Acropolis (Nueva Acrópolis) in Spain, during which time she expanded the cultural activity of this institution to more than 30 cities around the country. She has also coordinated the activities of New Acropolis in Europe.

After the death of the founder, Jorge Ángel Livraga, in 1991, she was elected International President of New Acropolis. In this capacity she was responsible for managing and coordinating the cultural and educational work of New Acropolis in all the countries in which this international association is established. Currently, she is the Honorary President of the International Organization New Acropolis.

She has written more than thirty books and handbooks about Practical Philosophy, Psychology, Ancient Civilizations, Astrology, etc., including the following:

The Everyday Hero (NA. Mumbai, 2018)

Philosophy for Living (NA. Mumbai, 2016)

What do we do with the Heart and the Mind? (NA. Bangalore, 2019)

Los Juegos de Maya (The Games of Maya) (Editorial NA. Madrid, 2001. 1st Ed. 1980).

Para Conocerse Mejor (Know Yourself Better) (Editorial NA. Madrid, 2015).

El Ideal Secreto de los Templarios (The Secret Ideal of the Templars) (Editorial NA. Madrid, 2015).

Several of her works have been translated into other languages in over 40 countries.

International Organization New Acropolis

New Acropolis is a worldwide non-profit organization, with centres in over fifty countries.

Established by Professor Jorge Angel Livraga on the foundations of practical philosophy and universal fraternity, New Acropolis is inspired by a fundamental respect for human dignity beyond differences of race, gender, culture, religion or socio-economic status. New Acropolis respects diversity but also tries to transcend it in search of a higher unity through shared universal ethical principles.

At New Acropolis, philosophy is more than just intellectual food for thought. We study philosophy as a means to integrate science, arts, ethics and metaphysics in order to work towards global human development.

This vision is implemented through a wide range of programmes that combine practical education with cultural and volunteering activities. New Acropolis also promotes an awareness of current affairs, both locally and globally, and focuses on improving the human condition by aligning ourselves with the laws of nature.

To learn more about New Acropolis, visit **www.acropolis.org**